By the same author:

For Revery *(a+bend press, 2000)*

Hate *(96 Tears Press, 1995)*

Mark Salerno

METHOD

The Figures

2002

Cover art by Robert Therrien, *No Title*, 2001.
Inkjet on paper on panel. 46 x 42 5/8 inches.
Courtesy of Gagosian Gallery. Photography by Rob McKeever.

Author photograph by Ted Williams.

Grateful acknowledgement is made to the editors of the following, where some of these works first appeared: *Angle, apex of the M, Arshile, Chicago Review, Denver Quarterly, The End Review, Explosive, First Intensity, Juxta, Situation, Talisman, VAN* (Canada), *Windover* and ZYZZYVA.

The epigraph is reprinted by permission of Robert Creeley and the publisher from "Thinking of Wallace Stevens" in *Echoes* (New York: New Directions, 1993).

The author wishes to acknowledge and thank the late William Bronk, the late Edward Dorn and Edward Brookner for their careful reading of this text in manuscript.

Distributed by Small Press Distribution, Berkeley, California.

The Figures, 5 Castle Hill, Great Barrington, Massachusetts 01230.
Copyright © 2002 by Mark Salerno
ISBN 1-930589-11-5

For Candace J. Eritano

Contents

In My Paintings / 13
Tranquility / 14
Grievous Angel / 15
Various / 16
Bob's Frolic / 17
Trading Fours / 18
Wrong Again / 19
Just ["Say he wanted a strange possession"] / 20
For William Bronk / 21
A Calendar of Days / 22
Recapitulation / 23
Method / 24
Recitative (Muse) / 25
A Dutch Door / 26
The Chinese New Year / 27
Phase One (In Which Doris Gets Her Oats) / 28
You Heard Me / 29
I See a Red Door / 30
Sorts / 31
Flush 'Em Out / 32
Reverie / 33
Just ["Morning drear the body's"] / 34
Apparent / 35
Shanghaied / 36
Honeyman / 37
Beveled / 38
Harsh / 39

It Is As If / 40
Midnight Train / 41
Does Not Win the West / 42
Dingus / 43
Three on the Tree / 44
Nothing Ventured / 45
Huckle Buck / 46
My Sharona / 47
A Small a Chinese Window / 48
Zip / 49
Nearly Twenty Years Have Passed / 50
Intimate / 51
Draggin' the Line / 52
Wait in the Car / 53
Yer Blues / 54
Tom's Number Five / 55
Vow / 56
Too Starsky / 57
Points / 58
Agent / 59
Extra / 60
Sum / 61
Like I Care / 62
Doubt / 63
Woody 'N You / 64
Match / 65
You Had a Good Job and You / 66
The Crown Collapsed / 67

The joy was always to know it was the joy,
to make all acquiesce to one's preeminent premise.

— Robert Creeley

Method

In My Paintings

In my paintings I am apt to find
the thousand injuries I had borne
if only a crude childlike hand a
glass half-full slash half-empty
questions lists key words and
observations of everyday life
my painting is my way and yet
I long for an art that would
be more than an expression of
my hatreds and desires as occurs
a congenial mode of thought for me
is counting granted conspiracies
granted the baseline of chance
and a small green tree obscuring.

Tranquility

What good would it do to state
one's regrets. That baleful list.
Oh captain, my suntan. My couch
of memory. Sprung June and skeins
of gauzy light. Dusk and longing.
The choked desires of people I
thought I could save. They wore
slacks they wore skirts they wore
hose and silk. Gone now as summer
beyond anyone's care and lost
in the rose light. What's left is
bitter, a world I always hated.

Grievous Angel

Before a list of images the scattered
say bits but isn't content very tiny
a gaudy even a messy fascination for
who would be stately or far-flung is
condemned by those who surround him
like the important modern before the
sticky animal versus moral nature
granted not paying very close granted
these shifting and polished surfaces
P. had said her breastal area and I
a lineman for the county I hear you
whose major theme in any case was
depictive for glowy so in my methods
and she a wanton she refuses to sum up.

Various

I'd wanted a speaking voice to go
if language only handles content
everywhere snares and delusions
the point being new rules in ten
years what will you believe for
an art and much too technical in
my methods these pieces seem to
let us review I thought of it as
my capture my things the way she
held herself poised the way she
so what if doorways to walk God
help us transitive windows are we
a messy fascination with what is
or repair to the adult of the human.

Bob's Frolic

We say we have a choice as if
but alls falls down and stories
that seemingly need to be told
a nervous tic peculiar to human
culture if words were joys she
says number them number each one
for all who fall make a record
ever after a girl gets "shanghaied"
in a movie or in real-life doings
these pieces seem to fit who cares
what really happened to lovers
who balked or got bored the thousand
injuries and in any case she refuses
to sum up her life experiences.

Trading Fours

Barren for broken so might as well
sky up in the not too distant thighs
O grievous angle these pieces seem
where a juncture of two like souls
might color in the planets and airy stars
it's a buddy movie the central character
I want my cowboys to sound like I think
cowboys should sound like in my methods
I loved the repeat the insistent and
anything technical shaping in my clutch
a falling apart heart animadversions
at the boat show in fact a boat load
here a more foreign sounding name
dirty dirty stage direction he sleeps.

Wrong Again

What had one so believed
to have arrived at gesture at
worn out body and so said
a language that seems only
to handle the world in ten
years what will you believe
this or everywhere snares
and delusions in my methods
the much too technical for
an art that would be more
in my clutch as these pieces
seem to fit but make which go
where what way would it matter
and who am I next time.

Just

Say he wanted a strange possession
and she a dream of stars or starlights
in the film the term is "shanghaied"
but what does that explain
I'd wanted a speaking voice to go
after afraid after tired and disoriented
whose blue outlines of hips and breasts
and so I humbled my mouth never farther
idiot don't write that down
let us review the writing on the wall
I thought of it as my capture my things
wherein even the poet-doctor finds his love
mired in regret for desire and if he runs off
with Julie Christie well who wouldn't.

For William Bronk

We look out fine and the world
so be it something followed by
something in any case not what
we think for who would be
thrown back or thought of even
the way her hands say or glowy
all young persons are beautiful
I'm speaking sir and when I talk
like cancels out like she resolves
this conflict by losing her mind
idiot don't write that down
O lonely trifle O desire
we look out upon the world and
we see something though.

A Calendar of Days

Moments in memory for they are
simultaneously clarifying and
obscuring as our experiences
of the real cast off or break
all persons when young their
choking balking or just didn't
and I who am apt to remember a
congenial mode for me was longing
O divan of recollection O color
idiot don't write that down
in the time too late the world
too far gone I'd wanted a no
more lonely company of persons
questions lists and key words.

Recapitulation

Wondered how far down to get
a simile is a mode of comparison
metaphor the same how far up
in my methods and so they are
from a small town originally
we thought of it as nature's
later a language that only
handles the world first you
splice no first you druggie
headlong into the chop chop
but let's a serious emotion
definition of serious blah blah
blah from whence I most did
and grace in a world gone.

Method

Scour the dross say
what seems real alive
you're alone O broken
hearted melody O fly
in the paradoxical ointment
a person is unevenly
loved and yet these
glinting and burnished
surfaces seem always to
tilt and throw back the
light without purpose
I admire that saving up
that scrupulously main-
tained day followed by
a next and a next when where
something else is then said.

Recitative (Muse)

I'd wanted a speaking voice to go down how
whose rills buck and stammer on the clear air
for in my methods one gets from here to there
she was beautiful blue outlines of hips and breasts
in the fading light and so I humbled my mouth
assuming all other variables and the baseline
lovers who balked or got bored with the promises
they made a little loose maybe wavering even
if only possession if only pushing out if only
in my paintings some content is a personal reference
to places or people I assume I will want to remember
a glimpse while never farther these pieces seem to fit
I'd wanted a speaking voice an airy charm
and for an art that would be more.

A Dutch Door

If I make my reports so be it
in detail in minute particulars
the vast array the ever-shifting
panorama and finest gradations
of felt experience my speaking
voice is not my only voice and
now I think of Gigi LaMorte lo
these many years traduced wronged
abandoned she was known as a pleasing
bit in the passing human cavalcade
a congenial mode of thought for me
in my methods for they are everywhere
apparent look back if you must and
so be it if I make my reports.

The Chinese New Year

The joy was always to know
one thinks of a recorded I
a model appropriate to
certificates or official papers
a knee-high version of self
and the others what were they
fine blue outlines stay one
song says linger the other
in my clutch never farther
not to be understood as
something taken but a promise
abjured O broken hearted
melody O simple bitter I give
you this always to know it was.

Phase One (In Which Doris Gets Her Oats)

Bitter for rowdy in my methods
don't compromise the system rather
move the background closer
to the foreground or say a
cavalcade of scattered bits
I liked my pieces too technical
for words that were hard to say
O simple bitter that's too harsh
in a young country longing to be
modern of my surfaces wrought of
parameters powdery in the dim like
a philosophical equivalent of the
boat show messy even the joys were
words for a no more lonely company.

You Heard Me

A tree in winter blunt roads
images and distorted facts
a pain that stops and starts
are you talking to me what
I'd wanted legs a body in my
clutch the whatever from whence
I most did take but unreliable
they left or got bored with the
swill between the lines but
what I believed was simple for
an art that would be more in
my methods these pieces seem
I mean I liked them even the
so often hard to say words.

I See a Red Door

That far road the trucks rumble
distantly down my messy fascin-
ation an insistent and a noisy O
I thought about all the sex parts
but she was irrational so the
subject was chaos it's a good one
built out of words I liked
the ambiance so what if clotted
all this misery over a mixed up was
like I care what your big daddy do
O lengthening light O couch of
mammary what I believed was simple
not so simple as time love money
and or grace in a world gone wrong.

Sorts

He is condemned and she refuses
simultaneously clarifying and obscuring
there's a window in the tree there's
a cup underneath the paint job I
thought you were you and I was me
O beveled glowy O injury
for my anxiety was to know I loved
within obvious limits a constant
reification I had borne as best I could
how the names brought everything back
and if I liked the way my pieces fit so
be it surface be it music vast and rowdy
an insistent particular noise of ours
in this messy drama of like upon like
I did what I had to do
you did what you wanted too.

Flush 'Em Out

In my paintings a congenial mode
to say in paragraphs in sentences
in words whence I most did take
O lovely light as winter lengthens
into the unified field theory
of spring I'd wanted legs or for
example money lots of it or for
example time more than I'll ever
have or for example what of love
a name locked away a destination
never to be reached an outstanding
debt left unhappily and unpaid a
simile a metaphor a transitive or a
street remembered in popular songs.

Reverie

The joy was always to know to sink
my teeth into bitter he expresses
her as someone with the power to
alleviate his heart and his mind
he expresses her as legs in my
methods I longed for an art for
a young country too late for all
you and your co-religionists
I'm going to flush them out a
little loose maybe wavering even
you are there I know you are of
the thousand injuries I had borne
a cast-off emotion a smug contempt
a know-it-all a valentine a someone.

Just

Morning drear the body's
gone hello I mark you
chunks of bitter in the
time before solace what
consubstantial other a
be here with me the lonely
pick up in a mixed up was
write them down right and
when they're gone all you
have is words by a kind
of lost process but so be it
they helped me O blank
and then again O and then
again the other thing a blank.

Apparent

Say what seems real but
you are always giving up
in your voice a note sir is
a note and it comes from
yeah yeah just sing the song
gave me permission to be
what I was a cast-off a
bitter think a know-it-all or
a valentine in the chop chop
stay says one song linger
the other but too technical
so a turning away he went out
to buy crime scene tape he went to
the boat show to the candy counter
I don't think he's coming back.

Shanghaied

Of the thousand injuries I had borne
I was charging but that light
gave me permission to be powdery
in the dim or messy to review then
a congenial mode of thought for me
was rowdy in my clutch whereas
my enemies for they are present
of smug contempt merely depictive
I'm gonna flush 'em out citizens
definition of the end of company
and merely human care so long I'd
wanted say a simple or a hand holding
whatever and if two people give up
while overhead the planets and
innumerable tiny stars.

Honeyman

There were things I said
a plangent insistent tone
to find my speaking voice
my glowy say in all this
sad ruckus who's happy I
kiss your palm who on a
day we were settle O couch
of definition for a wanton
and O lovely light I think
of Gigi LaMorte lo these
many years merely voiced
she was content with surface
I thought of as mine as my
own as in any case happens.

Beveled

What had one wanted so to be
edge of faint morning light
the dim grey over the high ridge
a tree in winter blunt roads
or someone's loving hand that
touched your hand everything's
here everything's now so be
of good cheer you there you with
the glasses on a beef bowl a
punch bowl what the hell it was
another transitive mode bright
stacks of meaningless elegance of
lines and scattered light
powdery in the dim the stars.

Harsh

Joy of shipwrecks joy of nothing
hellfire raining down from the sky
I'd like to see that one boxed-in
day after another grief the people
you failed or otherwise marred
"I mar you" for another transitive
not to mention their climates of
disease or terms they were caught
helpless within their movie got
weird so I went out to the candy
counter a decade whisks by and your
necktie flips it wasn't for others
what it was for me even the words
joys for a no more lonely company.

It Is As If

Broken rubble of blunt winter
a dead light out upon the far
in my paintings I longed for
counting tired of that I'd wanted
joys for a no more lonely not
this messy fascination a cast
off a merely wanton it's how
we came to the new world to be
modern to be not more than a
glimpse or whatever for glowy
flush them out you and your
hoople co-religionists another
bottomless pit of lost beliefs
to be thought of as longed for.

Midnight Train

Of the thousand injuries I had
too late for all O my tovarich
a beef bowl a punch bowl he is
remembering the death like an
essay about a poem about a man
of his only love lo these many years
it's a pain that stops and starts
after which mockery asks to be
paid sure go ahead it was bad
timing but he thought of it as a
life-style and so he expresses her
from whence I most did take for
all I was was glowy words and
everywhere the hand of the artist.

Does Not Win the West

Took a wrong turn maybe got lost
confronted unforeseen obstacles
granted mistakes were made granted
obstinate cynical unyielding one
might add bitter nonetheless
given the information available
in your voice why if you only
knew me in my methods every-
where present there are jumps
in information as if choppy
he is remembering the death of
a glimpse all that there is to
he is remembering content why
are you always congenial to me
that light was permission then
I really began the death of her
only one and you are always in
my clutch never done with did
you think I'd lay down did you
think I'd.

Dingus

We wish for what we cannot
have insistent even messy
a fascination for rowdy in
my methods I sometimes wish
I had a light hand like M.'s
a little loose maybe wavering
even scattered to be longing
in such a young country of my
wish to be congenial or no more
lonely or color drumming so
a definition of too late as one
might be blew it say done say time
all the while I thought it was just me
and this powdery drooping starlight.

Three on the Tree

We wish for what we cannot
a congenial mode of thought
lovers who balked or got bored
it all had to do with surface
possession anger a loose or
tightly fitted hate emotion
who would have thought a poet
a doctor freezing his ass off just
fourteen lines from the red army
for what we cannot glimpse
definition of desire he got
fed up with modern for technical
after which mockery like love.

Nothing Ventured

To start he is remembering
a glimpse a minute content
a theme with variations or
the important colon before
images and distorted facts
my voice my speaking voice
wanted joy wanted company
not this late and too far gone
possession anger or the hate
emotion even surfaces curves
he is attracted he is looking
for slow glowy in the powdery
given we wish for what we can-
not was it wrong a wrong wish.

Huckle Buck

Meet me as if to say may I
whatever the body wants
so be it give it prove it all
night definition of wants
another transitive mode a
way to get a note is a note
sir yeah yeah for scattered
in my clutch meet me there
in the fields behind the virgin
and the dynamo where words
were hard to say so number them
prove it to a counted measure
where is love where is every
snare and delusion where is.

My Sharona

What matters is sounds funny
for light they came here for
and so permission was given
here we take our pleasures slow
always to know it was the joy
idiot don't write that down
in the body in my clutch for
breasts and of the thousand
injuries thighs her name's
not what matters stay says
one song linger the other
in the time too late in my
voice I am always giving up
that is in my speaking voice.

A Small a Chinese Window

With us the disguise must be
complete don't write that down
his name's not a kind of call
a kind of yellow I was a face
pushing out words granted mean
granted insistent for a mixed
up and she a Kay Lenz type or
else so be it with us prompted
yet again toward a caviling a
like the important color before
a list of images to pulverize
the window in the tree the cup
underneath the paint job or say
what a grace with us might be.

Zip

With us the disguise sounds funny
I'd wanted joy wanted company not
the hate emotion but in my methods
always to know granted too harsh
granted the important colon before
my colon O son of memory like a
trumped-up was too late for all
a congenial mode of thought for me
is killing time with glowy words
what can you say about love before
a list takes over every aspect of
our environment stupid with injury
I wish I had a light hand like M.'s
I wish a reverie a beveled I wish.

Nearly Twenty Years Have Passed

Of the thousand injuries I had
with us the disguise must be
the dim grey over the high ridge
a little loose maybe wavering even
for who knew when young all
persons are beautiful were we
wrong to be alive or is this the
pronoun the hoax of modernism
a congenial mode for me was love
not your improbable hierarchies
I liked the arbitrary the technical and
anything that repeats for transitives
because there is not plot in painting
a pratfall to faint applause and exit.

Intimate

What had one wanted for a
certainty that say like the
moon look up and it's gone
nothing is positive about
art except that it is a word
poor looked at humans how
he thought of himself as an
Ernie Borgnine type and she
the messy fascination of a
thousand injuries of lovers
who balked or got bored with
I wonder how much more of this
I can take for crime scene tape
he went out to the candy the boat.

Draggin' the Line

Be done with it them arbitrary
or requisite in the time too
what of it say blank go on or
nothing is positive before a list
alive you're alone a little loose
who wanted the whatever persons
when young they were beautiful
am I never to abide beyond these
my own messy fascinations or and
what way would it matter in my
voice I am always it for my way
of being in the world of images
the hate emotion the I loved you
truth I took for topic for content.

Wait in the Car

With us what had or what's one
say we know I want for beveled
I want my paintings to look ugly
up close for the insistent whose
major theme was mere obsession
I loved the too technical surface
of women who fuss and men for
explanation or some lost beliefs
now all I do is destroy and so to
my enemies I wasn't always like
this with us this no more lonely
and the hate emotion it's only one of
several so what's one to do if go where
were we wrong and yes I was.

Yer Blues

A way is what I don't want
or who'll come for you now
women fuss with themselves
too much while men in every
snare and delusion where is
drag that over here why don't
you for bitter in my methods
gave me permission and a way
for rowdy loose that light
granted congenial granted a
lighter hand like M.'s from
whence I most did take a grace
for small and all too soon a way.

Tom's Number Five

For how was I to know all
young persons when young
only knew how or what if
you don't write that down
those were test questions
for glowy to be narrower
a record then a congenial
too technical that gets us
nowhere because who cares
or how could it matter we
are talking what happened
right or so be it I'd wanted
company in the glimpse hands
held and so a way to remember.

Vow

Of the thousand injuries I wonder
how much more there's no line with
these people you absolutely have to
flush them out so he gets wispy
here a definition of desire not to
say color drumming for possession
give 'em the gunsel what you heard
me for modern in a young country
longing to be glowy he went out
for crime scene tape he went to
the boat show not to say blah blah
blah idiot don't write that down
I'd wanted joy wanted company for
who would be stately or far-flung.

Too Starsky

They got me up and down for wasn't
I a twin born with fear my right
arm or in the sack or to hell fine
in a hand basket so be it for my
anxiety was to know the names and
without any other recourse except
in brochures supplied for free by
the government you just write and
they send them granted test questions
granted conspiracies or that like
for a mere ninety nautical miles
of what would be a first passage
until I was down to my Bardot once
taken for glowy from having been
the like agency of stars or starlight
of airy matters and of my soul's domain.

Points

How begin begin again
whose griefs I would
most assuage you can't
messy fascination one
day for how for a mixed
up was and next the next
there's blanks here it's
choppy the point being
different rules I love
loved you but my anxiety
was to know possession
a mere nautical ticker
tape busted confetti and
words that were hard to.

Agent

What might be said in the time
for what was central or even
who balked or got bored I like
a big painting to look small
for my anxiety to intimacy but
if she had blanks so be it all
persons when young love a semi-
colon a messy fascination with
whatever was in my clutch for
here say body names breasts or
thighs in any event a list of
images number them for soothing
present lovers who promised I
wonder how much more of this.

Extra

To write in a year a name for
a day granted a list of images
granted the female and of body
of ways to remember content but
what if wanton what if messy I
most did take to be thought of
when young all persons are the
whatever balked or got bored
I wonder how much more of this
to have arrived in worn out body
powdery in the dim was a kind
of light for permission of what
came more from other paintings to
make you and yes I have no message
the words were hard to say names.

Sum

A little farther into the blue the
chop chop I wonder how much
for lovers who balked or got
permission then bitter for rowdy
cream smooth my mere obsession
so every snare and delusion far
more I can take in my clutch in
my methods definition of desire
not to say sticky scattered bits
O lost beliefs O glowy like being
shanghaied to the surface color
and all my anxieties in the time
for a way to remember the world
far gone as well as the people.

Like I Care

In my younger and more vulnerable
the highest spiritual aspiration
yet rowdy for bitter for loose
not to mention my anxiety for a
proximate a more congenial how
that would be so like my voice
that is to say my speaking voice
with which to conjure airy matters
if wrong I wonder how much more
your messy fascination falls open
your love your dupe or was it the
hoax of modernism again a glimpse
pushing out words being the point
if you only knew me blah blah blah.

Doubt

If you only ventured upon
O briefest reverie O balky
of pushing out words so certainly
made use of that trope as with
a paradoxical a merely wanton
loyalty to the past where was
the granted messy fascination
granted rowdy for bitter as if
wrong I wonder depictive the
counting whence I most did take
my anxiety was to remember gaudy
flecks in the little new world
and glowy could I never be other
if only you say I wasn't.

Woody 'N You

When the air of the arbitrary
vanishes and we fall into
positions that feel destined
stay says one song linger the
other if only you knew me a
plaintive to make the disguise
complete granted shanghaied
granted whatever I was down to
remember if wrong so be it that
time not draw the color from
words pushing out messy whence
I most in my voice say she was
powdery in the dim or how else
vanish into air and wispy stars.

Match

Before a list say follow whom
returned compulsively to the
same themes yet and yet spare
light pale into the clear air
a company then in the world
granted too late granted too
far gone her point being
different rules so quit your
whining mere obsession to be
thought of as content so that
time not draw the color from
an optimist an optometrist
curses insults vows promises
as well as other hard to say words.

You Had a Good Job and You

Like in a shipwreck we are alone
a watery and embarrassed simile
I longed for an art that would be
more good sir for how else am I
to speak of airy matters or the
thousand injuries I had borne
people you know get tired of a
sign system in which the erotic
is obscured we thought of it as
congenial as nature's toothbrush
idiot don't write that down
preposition modes of comparison
they balked or got bored on sore feet
after a long day at say the boat show.

The Crown Collapsed

A congenial mode of thought for
me is drumming there is not plot
in painting so that time not draw
the color from how much more if
wrong loose if wavering modern
my heart a hoax of mere obsession
I love I miss blah blah blah
the central character in the film
for an art that would be more
of reverie surface or glowy beveled
the joy was hard to say words and
delusions to be thought of as desire
the way her hands say or the simple
small-town in a world gone wrong.

Mark Salerno was born in New York City in 1956. He is the author of *Hate* (96 Tears Press, 1995) and *For Revery* (a+bend press, 2000). His work has appeared in numerous distinguished journals, including *Exquisite Corpse, Fell Swoop, Jejune* (The Czech Republic), *Mirage Period(ical), Ribot, Skanky Possum* and *sub-TERRAIN* (Canada). He lives in Hollywood, where he edits *Arshile: A Magazine of the Arts*.

Method was set in 10 point
Palatino with 12.5 heads and printed in
an edition of 750 at Sharp Offset Printing, Inc., Rutland,
Vermont, of which ten are numbered
in Roman Numerals I — X
& signed by the poet,
January 2002.